The
Wilderness
Experience

WOMEN IN WILDERNESS

WRITINGS AND PHOTOGRAPHS

SELECTED AND EDITED BY

SUSAN & ANN ZWINGER

A Harvest Original

HARCOURT BRACE & COMPANY

SAN DIEGO • NEW YORK • LONDON

A TEHABI BOOK

Gabrielle Daniels, "A City Girl Discovers the Forest," excerpt reprinted from *Another Wilderness: New Outdoor Writing by Women,* edited by Susan Fox Rogers (Seal Press, Seattle, 1994) with permission of the publisher.

Jan DeBlieu, excerpt from *Hatteras Journal* by Jan DeBlieu, © 1987. Fulcrum Publishing, Golden, Colorado; 800-992-2908.

Gretel Ehrlich, excerpt reprinted from *The Solace of Open Spaces,* © 1985 by Gretel Ehrlich. Used by permission of Viking Penguin, a division of Penguin Books USA Inc., and author's agent, Darhansoff and Verrill, Literary Agency.

Cathy Johnson, excerpt reprinted from *On Becoming Lost: A Naturalist's Search for Meaning* by Cathy Johnson, copyright © 1990. Gibbs Smith, Publisher. Used by permission of author.

Margaret E. Murie, excerpt from *Two in the Far North* by Margaret E. Murie. Copyright © 1957, 1962, and 1978 by Margaret E. Murie. Reprinted with permission of Alaska Northwest Books™.

Vera Norwood, reprinted from *Made from this Earth: American Women and Nature* by Vera Norwood. Copyright © 1993 by the University of North Carolina Press, 1993. Used by permission of the publisher.

Terry Tempest Williams, from *An Unspoken Hunger* by Terry Tempest Williams. Copyright © 1994 by Terry Tempest Williams. Reprinted by permission of Pantheon Books, a division of Random House, Inc., and by author's agent Brandt & Brandt Literary Agency.

Library of Congress Cataloging-in-Publication Data
Women in wilderness: writings and photographs/selected and edited
    by Susan and Ann Zwinger; photographs by award-winning women photographers.
        p.   cm. — (The Wilderness experience)
   "A Tehabi book."
   ISBN 0-15-600224-8 (pbk.)
    1. Natural history—United States. 2. Women naturalists—United States—Biography.
  3. Naturalists—United States—Biography. 4. Natural history—United States—Pictorial works.
  I. Zwinger, Susan, 1947- . II. Zwinger, Ann. III. Series.
  QH104.W65 1995
  508.73´092´2—dc20   95-12538
  [B]

Women in Wilderness was produced by Tehabi Books. Nancy Cash–*Series Editor and Developmental Editor*; Laura Georgakakos–*Manuscript Editor*; Sam Lewis–*Project Art Director*; Andy Lewis–*Art Director*; Tom Lewis–*Editorial and Design Director*; Sharon Lewis–*Controller*; Chris Capen–*President.*

Harcourt Brace & Company and Tehabi Books, in association with The Basic Foundation, a not-for-profit organization whose primary mission is reforestation, will facilitate the planting of two trees for every one tree used in the manufacture of this book. This edition is printed on acid-free paper that meets the American National Standards Institute Z39.48 Standard.

Printed in Hong Kong through Mandarin Offset.
First edition 1995
A B C D E

CONTENTS

WOMEN IN WILDERNESS

We chose these selections on women and wilderness after endless animated and absorbed conversations—by an alpine tarn wreathed with wildflowers in the Yosemite wilderness, on a wild Pacific beach beneath an Olympic Peninsula rainforest, at home over cups of tea beside the computer.

Women traditionally have created gardens, learned plant names, and listened to the earth. They often express their connection to the natural world through human relationships, through raising children, for example, teaching them to love and respect the wilderness. For many women the experience itself is sufficient and they do not feel the need to write about it.

Still, there is an impressive body of writing from women who celebrate their attachment to the natural world through words. We have been reassured and delighted that women are such excellent and astute observers, such beautiful and vivid writers, carriers of the message that this is a wondrous and marvelous natural world. This wealth of writing results in part from the changes of the last three decades, changes both in women's roles and in Americans' alliance with nature. The feminist movement, an increasing emphasis on physical well-being, greater acceptance of women participating in outdoor activities, and innovations in gear that have lightened the physical load, have all contributed to women moving more freely in the out-of-doors. They are more easily finding paths into a natural world that is apart from their everyday lives of family and friends and the often repetitive duties of work. For many, meeting the wilderness head-on has changed their lives. As Gretel Ehrlich writes in *The Solace of Open Spaces,* "I suspect that my original motive for coming here [Wyoming] was to 'lose myself' in new and unpopulated territory. Instead of producing the numbness I thought I wanted, life on the sheep ranch woke me up. The vitality of the people I was working with flushed out what had become a hallucinatory rawness inside me. I threw away my clothes and bought new ones; I cut my hair. The arid country was a clean slate. Its absolute indifference steadied me."

Many writers, like Ehrlich, are able to vividly capture our attention as readers, to share

1

their knowledge of the natural world and the passion of their encounters, to carry us into their immediate experience of the deep and primary relationship that combines empathy, respect, and understanding.

Beyond superb writing, we deliberately chose essays from different parts of the country, a broad range of approach and experience, age and race. The variety of settings reveals how specific place affects both perception and writing style. But the breadth of these writings also serves to emphasize the universality of women's experience in wilderness. Despite the differences in age, place, and style, their message is bell-like and clear: wilderness is an essential part of their lives.

We chose selections to illustrate the width of the wilderness experience from Jan DeBlieu's Atlantic Coast to Margaret Murie's celebration of the wilds of Alaska. The broad places in-between may seem less dramatic, but wilderness is there nevertheless, as in Cathy Johnson's Missouri landscape. Water sparkling with meaning runs through these selections in the essays of Terry Tempest Williams, Jan DeBlieu and Cathy Johnson. Gabrielle Daniels speaks with the voice of a young, urban African-American discovering the forest and moving through it to a feeling of home in a new and vastly different world.

The writers range in age from Margaret Murie, born in 1902, to Terry Tempest Williams, the youngest of the writers here and, fittingly, a friend of Murie's. This age range allows us to see how things have changed over time. The concept of women in wilderness was once an oxymoron; Murie reminds us that the only acceptable way women could once enter the wilderness was with a man. Today, the concept of women in wilderness is no longer so unsettling.

We have been intrigued by the different ways in which women came to feel at home in the wilderness. Daniels, speaking from an urban background, discovered with astonishment her pleasure in wilderness. Others, like Murie and many of her generation, went out with loved ones, saw wilderness through others' eyes and came, over time, to develop their own confidence and understanding. Terry Tempest Williams grew up with a grandparent who took her out to watch birds. Cathy Johnson drew and painted wild places for pleasure, becoming so fascinated by her subjects that she became a first-rate naturalist. Gretel Ehrlich went in desperation, as many do, seeking solace after overwhelming loss. Some stay close to home, daily recording the nuances of their surrounding landscape and its health with such depth and care and charm that their record becomes an eloquent and elegant one. Some of us were so intrigued with the workings of the natural world that staying out became the passport to learning and research.

Only recently have Anglo women gone out alone. "Going back" to wilderness is a mystery to Native American women who've never left and for whom life is inextricably linked to the natural world that nourishes them, that has given them legends and reasons and ceremonies. They have long gone out on vision quests and to gather food or medicinal plants. Their relationship to wilderness is often revealed through stories and myths rather than essays. Robin Tekwelus Youngblood, a writer and an artist, beautifully expresses an integrity of psyche and place.

Above all, these seven women, chosen from many wonderful writers, go out there. They record furiously. They celebrate the wild and healthy life they find around and within themselves. They choose to be "out there" because they want to be, and they write directly about being there. They are writers who have ventured past known, safe edges to glimpse a different reality.

Throughout history, women have been defined by their relationships, and stepping out of traditional roles seems dangerous to many. But difficult as it is to come by, solitude is a necessary part of our relationship to wilderness. It is in solitude, so newly available to women, that we find self-definition and value. This numinous yet immediate sense of one's place is ultimately one of the most empowering experiences in life.

Woman's connection to wildness is deep, long-term, and unique. Within these pensive, daily encounters lies a key for maintaining quality life on the planet. An attunement remains that once ensured their infants' or tribes' survival, an attunement to nuance, texture, a sudden shift of wind, the gesture of an animal. Women are superb observers; every fiber of female being is conditioned to notice particulars. We are recorders of subtlety, celebrators of both small detail and gigantic phenomena. This creates in us a desire to keep these phenomena safe and thriving; creates a passion for the entire ecosystem in all its intricate workings.

This work has made the two of us, who write and draw our own lives, thankfully at home in the wilderness world, joined in spirit to those who listen to bees bustle among the larkspur, who hear wind nudge the pine needles, and who inhale the scent of wilderness in the air. —*Susan Zwinger & Ann Zwinger*

INTO WILD PLACES

I have been close to wild places from the moment I could walk but my mother has not, and her transition amazes me. As I was growing up, I knew her only as a full-time mother. For years her creativity found outlet, as many women's did and do, in volunteer work, cooking, and sewing most of our clothes.

After years away from art work, she began drawing again. The drawing led directly to her close examination of the plants and animals on our newly purchased land at 8,500 feet in the Rocky Mountains. Her letters to me at college raved about ecosystems, hydras, weasels, and puffballs. About the time most mothers are suffering empty-nest syndrome, she was drawing nests, studying the birds that lived in them, and capturing the insects on which they dined.

Then came the genesis of a life change which none of us could have anticipated. Rachel Carson's agent, Marie Rodell, visiting a mutual friend in Colorado Springs, sought a foray up into the mountains and my mother obliged her. Somewhere along the way, chatting about the Colorado landscape, she asked my mother if she would be interested in writing a book on Colorado ecology and Beyond the Aspen Grove *was born.*

What Ann Zwinger describes in this essay is her immersion into the wonders of the natural world. It is her way of keeping alive and inspired, young and healthy and energetic. It is an inspiration to all women: we can leap from fear of grasshoppers to entomology classes to dangerous desert isolation to whitewater canyons. We can, we must, leap everywhere we dream. —S. Z.

Nobody Here but Us Chitons by

ANN ZWINGER

I sit on a large but quite uncomfortable boulder, keeping an eye on the surges of water as they spread across the ledge around me and watching for a ravaging, returning tide. Susan has brought me here to Rialto Beach on the Olympic Peninsula on the morning of the lowest tide of the year, hurried me out here so I could see shelves and sea plants and pools normally covered. From where I sit I cannot see her and this pleases me: nobody here but us chitons. Not that I love Susan less, but that I crave solitude more.

My first experience in the honest-to-God outdoors came when I'd already had three children. Our family acquired land in the foothills of the Front Range of the Rocky Mountains. When a deer mouse jumped on our tent in the middle of the night it scared me to death, but it also piqued my curiosity. That curiosity led by circuitous route and incredible good luck to my writing a book about what a city girl found in that wonderful new world. The endless questions I asked then still animate my journeys and ballast my writing.

In the years since, my career as a natural history writer has taken me in widening circles from that place of heart and home. In a strange way, writing natural history has widened my sense of home; even after only ten minutes on a remote island off Chile I was "home." The small knowledge I carry with me, along with clean socks and a water filter, gives me an entree even into the most alien place—a green leaf is still a leaf, a fish is still a fish, and water still runs downhill.

My profession provides me with the most appropriate life possible: a reason to be out and a reason to learn. My connection with wilderness is only partly for solace or escape from the city. It is my livelihood, the work that defines my life. Being a natural history writer legitimizes the childhood yearning to stay out and play after all the other kids had gone indoors. It enables me to run rivers and fill my pockets with river pebbles, each an essay in itself.

One does not make one's living as a natural history writer: one makes one's life as a natural history writer. My insatiable curiosity drives me into the natural world where I find all the things that fascinate me and many things that stabilize me, where there is so much to learn about and so many larger rhythms to tune into. I also go out because of a growing need for solitude, a realization that I am not separate from nature but part of it. Not that solitude is always easy to arrange. People still look horrified when they find out where I'm going, what I'm doing. "You're *what?*" they say with disbelief and horror. But rivers run in my veins, I have brain coral in my head, the swish of the tides mark my inner turnings, the continually shifting swash line marks the vagaries of living. I don't like being cold, wet, tired, and hungry, but the irony is that being so evokes qualities of endurance I didn't know I had, it concentrates my powers of observation and intensifies the experience. It rearranges my relationship to the natural world and generates a different approach to thinking and to writing.

My agenda rarely changes. First, set up housekeeping—not a female thing at all, it's what Daniel Defoe had Robinson Crusoe do first. Once the mundane minimum is taken care of, I'm free to roam my kingdom, eat twice a day, go to sleep at dusk, and rise with dawn. I mark the turning of the earth, the brightening of the sky, the sound of a leaf falling, the tromp of ants carrying food back to their tiny volcano-shaped pile of dirt at my feet.

I am most conscious of listening when I go out alone, walking the Honaker Trail and sleeping by the San Juan River, counting desert bighorn sheep on the border of Arizona and Mexico, playing Robinson Crusoe in the Juan

Fernandez Islands, providing fodder for the myriad mosquitoes on the Outer Banks of South Carolina. Father DeSmet, traveling alone across the northern stretches of this continent in the eighteenth century, wrote, "Solitude seems to give scope to man's intellectual faculties; the mind seems more vigorous, the thought clearer."

This morning this shelf at the edge of the Pacific Ocean, with all its coming and goings, intrigues me: the lined chiton, the grazing urchin, the darting worm, the diaphanous nudibranch undulating like a snippet of silky chiffon in the water. But that's not enough. I need to know who this creature is, to hang a lovely Latin name on it that will open the doors of why it's here, what it's doing, where it began, and where it's going. The waves splash closer and I wonder how such a gossamer creature survives in a small pool when tons of water dump on it.

The incoming tide hurries me to shore. Such a sparse, tough landscape. But these are the intringing ones, where plants and animals teeter on the brink, the alpine tundra and the desert reaches where adaptations are sharp and driving. As one of those organisms paddling its way through survival, I find the personal responsibility of solitude and survival hangs a different edge on life. To perceive, to learn those adjustments, entices my head and my heart, and I do not come out by the same door wherein I went. ❀

NATURAL CONNECTIONS

While I covet rare time in the field spent alone, I also cherish the time spent with my marvelous daughter. She is a generous and articulate teacher. We share many outdoor memories and wilderness is the fabric onto which we embroider our experiences. Our relationship as mother and daughter and as friends has evolved from a wander across an Arkansas field when she was a little girl, to hours spent leaning over a tidal pool in Baja California, to long treks lugging backpacks through high altitude fellfields just months ago. We were camped at 10,500 feet near timberline, alongside a stream. On this trip, which included Susan's birthday, we raised a toast of freshly filtered, very cold stream water to the pleasures of wilderness and the vagaries that brought us there.

I inherited my wilderness genes from my daughter. It was she who first did wilderness camping, it was she who first went into the wilderness of Utah and came back beaming, it was she who drove alone to Alaska. From her experience and sturdy outlook I have taken courage and encouragement, both words from the Middle English root meaning "heart." Susan brought me up from a very timorous housewife to a rabid seeker of solitude.

Susan's track is different from mine for we are separated by a generation. "Ecology" was not in my vocabulary until college. "Environmentalism" didn't arrive until Earth Day, 1970. Susan grew up realizing that there were some knotty environmental dilemmas that her generation was going to have to solve. She does not waste time on blame but moves quickly and works hard to better conditions, especially those that are still salvageable. She has endured threats, something I've never had to do (my worst epithet is the little-old-lady-in-tennis shoes curse and being negated because I'm a woman). Because of Susan, I have a sharper view of the world today. She is an activist, poet, and artist, an indefatigable writer, and lecturer on such problem areas as old growth forests. Her words and thoughts are not mine, nor should they be, nor could they be, but in them I see my hopes and dreams and ideals. —A. Z.

Whacked Upside the Soul by

SUSAN ZWINGER

Seconds after I climb down the six-foot roots of a beached log, a high tide wave from the Pacific Ocean explodes nearby. The water shoots forty feet into the air, surging under the log pile and foaming down the other side of the spit. I cower like a small vole, unprepared for the fear that shoots up from the soles of my feet.

All in a naturalist's day's work.

I am driven to write about the natural world because I love it and because I want to heighten Americans' awareness of it. To me, it is a national tragedy that as we've become more urban, our connections to the wilderness—to the source of all life, food, medicines, spiritual nourishment, play, and exploration—are being forgotten.

I go far out into places where human beings are small and insignificant to sense my place in them. I go out most often alone, seeking closeness to a very elemental power. I sit near the thundering waves in winter at the highest of high tides in the Pacific. I watch the roaring black water cascading down precipitous black stone on a mountaintop in Alaska. I seek the unfamiliar immense expanses, hoping that they will slam into my consciousness as segments of the Earth's crust slam into one another. My writing is the faulting and uplift, the earthquake and vulcanism that result from such interface.

I go out into the humble, the intimate, the subtle wild places closer to home. In a nearby forest, within a few square feet I find mounds of moss and lichen and liverwort. Whenever I feel confined or blue, I go out to watch the world inventing itself anew. The human eye is a peculiar organism—at first it sees nothing, then a little, and then such an abundance that I lose all sense of tiny self and am swept into the wondrous infinity of life.

I am drawn, as my mother is, to the critical edges of life, be they warm test tubes of tidal pools or harsh expanses of Arctic tundra. Whenever I need a good whack upside the soul, I go to Earth's extremes and study the politics of survival. I love to imagine life beginning in these highly improbable conditions, in difficult crevices of rock and sea. I imagine myself a part of those amino acids which so suddenly glowed, organized, and slithered out of the mud pool.

I find wildness without even leaving home. The night sky above my apartment is filled with so many connect-the-dot mythological creatures and heavenly bodies that I cannot help but feel closer to the source of all life. The human urge to name, to categorize, to sort and explain falls away, and I gaze upward with a primitive awe.

I go out into the wilderness to be shocked, to be surprised into alertness. Once, walking along in Denali National Park, head down, unaware of my surroundings, I was terrified by what sounded like the sudden roar of a locomotive. A nine-foot wall of steely water burst toward me down a dry river channel. It was bizarre to watch the snout of a river move toward me like a train. High enough alongside its path, I was safe to watch the icy surge of water melt and bulldoze its way through the boulder wreckage of the last ice-dam burst. I stood alone with no one to explain this sight to me, but too enthralled to want to dissect it with the dull blade of language.

I go into wilderness to bear the burden of too much beauty. I believe the urge to seek out beauty will be the salvation of a healthy planet. There is nothing like the exquisiteness and strength of the natural world—in size, in multiplicity, in amplification, in subtlety. It demands both attunement and atonement. Often as I drive along Saratoga Passage, or along the Pacific Ocean in winter storm, or along Turnagain Arm, I wonder how it is that some appreciate the beauty in nature while others appreciate only its potential to profit a few.

I go out to record and research and celebrate those intricate loops of energy that are recycling through Nature's black box into more and more complex life forms. Mushrooms, for example, are fundamental to the forest's economy, nurturing and stabilizing the roots of new trees, releasing organic material from once-living plants into the soil as nutrients for future plants. Nothing is wasted in fungal activity. Everything dead is once again brought to life through the soil's mysteries.

Each woman goes out into the wilderness at a different level—from hanging from rock faces by one's toes, to barreling down dangerous whitewater, to quietly studying an insect going about its curiously wonderful business. For so long, unfounded fears and cultural propriety have imprisoned us in static, man-made rooms. Not going out at all is not an option if we are to remain healthy. We can no longer afford to live by unfounded fears.

Our humanity and womanhood are grounded in and amplified by our contact with wilderness. Those of us who keep field journals, however elaborate or simple, have found that these notebooks start the dark alchemy in which fact, sweat, and fond memory ferment and develop into a psychic perfume to be applied for years and years. ❧

A Sense
of Being

Cathy Johnson reminds us in her essay that the heart of wilderness may not be in faraway places with strange sounding names, but just down the road close to home. One might not think of the small midwestern town of Excelsior Springs, Missouri, as wilderness, but Johnson finds it there and delineates it in both words and paintings. Simply by taking a different point of view—lying on her back and looking up at the trees, for instance—Johnson finds a whole new world of patterns and proposals.

Trained as a professional artist and the author of many books on how to draw and paint in the out-of-doors, her watercolors are wilderness essays in themselves. Her words round out the image of the wilderness that is all about us just for the quiet looking. Her first book was called, prophetically enough, The Local Wilderness.

In this passage from Becoming Lost: A Naturalist's Search for Meaning, *Johnson reaches back to childhood, as many nature writers do, to recall the fresh enthusiasm and eagerness with which children view the world about them. She invokes the universal memory of what it was like to be an awestruck child and then weaves it back into our adult experience. Her description of wilderness brings back to us that first intense pang of wonder at those inexplicable dancing lights that kept back the dark, lights that warmed us and enchanted us, created by a parent who could make magic. —A. Z.*

Excerpts from *On Becoming Lost: A Naturalist's Search for Meaning* by

CATHY JOHNSON

In the cool water where my pale feet paddle, a crowd gathers. Shiners nibble at my toes; giant water striders canoe themselves effortlessly back and forth above them, their feet dimpling the surface film. Damselflies-times-two stand upside down in the still, mirrored surface of the pool; a few yards away the dense mat of water willows is alive with them. A small colony of algae forms on the fine hairs of my feet; have I been here so long? The spiders are already tying me immobile to

29

the rock where I sit; I am no different to them than a limestone boulder. A tiny butterfly has stopped to lay its eggs on my shoulder; I must stay here, then, until they hatch.

The coolness of the creek has entered my blood; it circulates in my veins, looping through me endlessly. My flesh has lost its florid heat at last; it is cool and pale. My heart pumps coolness; my mind thinks cool, easy summer thoughts, like peaches.

The tiny turbulence of the riffle where I sit is in total confusion; no one could follow the water's changing patterns for more than a second or two. Just as I think I have it mapped, it changes. But where I blur my eyes, withdrawing concentrating into myself, I see the pattern clearly, as if it were frozen in time. There is a reason for those repeated, interlaced V's strung out downstream, crossing, entangling, catching skylight like pale blue ribbons on a watery Maypole.

Downstream something is feeding; small fish, perhaps, or frogs. I see their silver splashes as they leap from the water like salmon. They ignore me as if I were only another rock.

And then I become aware of another V in the water; something is swimming toward me. Is it the snake I saw here last week? No, too large. Is it the snapping turtle, swimming purposefully upstream, head held out of the water? Not likely. I turn to stone, barely breathing: it is the muskrat that lives by the bridge. I see his wet black nose, nostrils flared above the water. His wake ribbons out behind him, sinuous and twisting. Surely he will see me—five yards, four yards, two. He is beyond swimming, now the stream is too shallow—he half-waddles, half-paddles towards me, totally unaware of my presence. His eyes must be as nearsighted as my own—or his concentration as intense. My legs block half the open water between the two big rocks; all of the shrunken summer river flows between my extended feet and the boulder on the other side, squeezed into less than a yard—surely he will turn aside, surely he will see me. He is close enough now to see the water beaded on his short, black eyelashes; I do not breathe. His fur is wet, stuck together in glossy, bicolored points, shining with the creek's wetness. I am a rock. He is a yard from me, twenty inches, twelve—he brushes my toes as he passes upstream!

I have never felt anything so vital. His sides are cool and round; I sense the warmth under that thick silk. I feel his sudden alarm, his surprise. I see the flash of white as his eyes go wide; he is as startled as I. He is galvanized, electric; he shoots the remaining three feet through the narrow passage as if on underwater wings and dives deep below the surface of the pool.

I exhale at last and see that he has done the same; silver bubbles mark his passage as he retreats upstream, never stopping to up periscope until he reaches the far end of the pool fifty yards away.

There are tears behind my eyes; my throat is constricted. I have what I have come for; I have lost myself—if only for an instant—and become something wholly other. I am grateful to the spirit of this place. I have become a part of this magic. . . .

·   ·   ·

Lying on my back on the picnic table's bench, a whole new world opens up before my eyes. Far overhead the tops of the trees are a moving mosaic of light and shade and translucent color, as if someone had pasted shards of glass on the wind. The oak leaves glow an almost neon green as the light passes through them, sharply delineating midrib and veins even at the tops of the trees, etching them dark as ink. The layer of cells at the outer edges of the leaves, the cells without chlorophyll, gives each an outline of bright sunlight. The cells within look crystalline, granular, as if I could walk between them; they sparkle with a cool green light like stars seen underwater. The light that falls on my face is cool and green too, moving like the watered silk of reflections under a bridge.

The lower leaves have provided food for a million hungry bugs, especially those of the lone box elder in the forest of oaks and hickories. The leaves of *Acer negundo* are shot full of holes, rustling in the breeze like ripstop nylon. The highest leaves look virtually untouched, undamaged. The territory of the leaf-eaters must be barely understory-high.

The sun sails directly overhead, but my eyes are shaded from the glare by a thick leaf cover, dense as a mat of water willows. Only those bright leaf edges cut my retinas, like knives. Between the trees the rays break through in long, reaching fingers, as if they would invite me up and away, through the layered leaves. I decline the invitation; I am strangely at peace here. From my protected vantage point, flat on my back and dreaming, I can see in that bright opening a passing army of dust motes and pollen grains like pale, moving smoke, drifting slowing through the woods. West to east, west to east, the army passes endlessly in review; I salute it drowsily without moving.

Larger specks of light, dancing erratically and against the prevailing wind, are the wings of small, flying insects, turned to fire by the sun. If they fly too close they'll burn like a moth at a candle flame, spiraling into the light; but these lazy dancers seem unconcerned—they've no plans to escalate to danger levels. They bob and float and spin like a company of Renaissance jesters. I wish I could go along, but I am pushed back by fingers of light, overcome by a wonderful weakness, dizzy with a profound peace.

My new vantage point, flat out and oddly attentive, gives me fresh eyes. From here I can imagine an earthworm's view of the massive trees rising all around me; their tangled skein of roots and soaring trunks are home and familiar to him in his cool burrow, sweet with leaf mold and the action of microscopic actinomycetes.

I can tell the direction of the gentle wind, unfelt in my protected position on the beach; I feel the glow of green light as well as see it; I watch the bright dust moving through the interstices of the trees. To the worm such a world is old hat, everything racing upward in an extreme perspective, racing up and away; it hardly rates a glance—if earthworms bother to glance.

I look beneath the picnic table to find two *Catocala* moths flattening themselves against the old wood, waiting for the night. Their bright underwings are hidden against the day under mottled cloaks of camouflage; it's as effective here on the weathered table as on the trunks of hickory and oak. I'd never have found them if I weren't wearing new eyes, if my awareness were not heightened by the looking. A bobbing, floating, rising, falling, turning ball of midges moves, ghostlike, through the trees; no wonder people see spirits in the deep wood. If I were younger—or more fanciful still—I'd give this light-ball a different sort of light, a corporate sensibility owned among the midges; imbue it with feeling, ask it its story, suspect it of a wood sprite's benevolence. I'd dance with it, ride it, wrap myself in it like a sentimental cloak of secrets, wear it like a living tiara, one that might whisper to me of lights and movement and what happens in the deep wood when I am not there to see. I'd find a mystery made of truth, cherubim about in broad daylight, the Creator in the creation.

I have loved—extravagantly, inexplicably—this small piece of earth. It's a fierce and exultant love, a love that frightens me with its strength at times—at once darkly atavistic, tribal, rooted in the earth like the oak and hickory forests that grow in this northwest Missouri country, and as full of light as a nova.

I have a great capacity for appreciation, for contentment—I *know* when I am at peace. As an almost-only child (my sister was grown and married before I was old enough to do much more than dress myself), I spent time alone and learned to love it. I like my own company; experience seems purer when undiluted by distraction.

I have walked these woods paths with a full and varied appreciation of my place in time, my solitude, my silence in a world noisy with rushing water and the crash of falling branches on a stormy midwestern afternoon, when tornado sirens must be imminent. It's as if I've ceased to be separate at last; I can't hear my own voice against that of the storm.

I have sat wrapped in an opera cloak of silence as I listened to the symphony of a small riffle in the Fishing River—listened and shared and played my part by simply being there, an audience of one.

I have felt love like a force—a strange love of landscape itself, of the earth beneath my feet—welling up and overflowing and exploding along the capillaries of my brain until I wanted to run free, not stopping until I could run no more, until I dropped like a stone and lay in place until the next glacier moved me.

There are times when I cannot believe I *am* separate from this earth, when I could swear the wind blows through me as it does the woven needles of the pine tree by the creek, when I feel my feet planted deep in the earth with the roots of trees and wildflowers, drawing sustenance. The hills shelter me.

Home. The word calls up images of sanctuary; a safe nest. But home needn't have four walls to fit that definition. I leave my walled and mortgaged home for one with a blue, domed ceiling and walls of open space. My real home expands as far as I can see; my arms reach out and encounter no boundaries—or perhaps come upon the solid, timeless rock that forms the knobby backbone of these northern Missouri hills.

.   .   .

The anachronistic circle of firelight is small and private—intimate. It carves an ephemeral den of flickering light, tucked into a green pocket of oak and hickory woods. I eschew the hissing, clanking glare of a gas lantern that reaches bold fingers of light far beyond the campsite and into everybody's business. The glow of firelight is perfect—modest, circumspect. Safe. I can see only the closest of the leaves, those picked out of darkness by the low light, but I am at home; I know these trees by sound and scent as well as by sight. The hail of hickory nuts on our tent, the slight tang of hickories and walnuts, the rich, mellow, woody scent of white oaks; I need little light for the braille of woods I've known since childhood.

The flame itself is home and magnet. Fire warms us when the sun deserts these wooded hills and drives away the night dampness; it cooks our food to smoky perfection and heats our washing water; it defines the perimeters of our temporary claim on the night and draws us home like hunger. It becomes a part of me again, a part of my life; it is as necessary as air.

Fire is a chaos-theory illustration of wild, unchartable patterns while owning, itself, a kind of immutable logic; there is a repetition that invites reverie. I contemplate the chemistry of combustion—the exchange of gases for heat, the leaving of log-shaped forms of gray, powdery ash that crumble at a touch like an ancient keepsake. It is a strange kind of alchemy, a closed circle of barter in which we have no part—unless we want it.

Soot burning invisibly within the flame lights my campsite; the blackened bottoms of my pots prove these carbon atoms are present in plenty. Fuel, heat, oxygen—it is the elemental formula for fire, but as changeable as need. Go heavy on the oxygen and the result is heat. Mix in a stout dose of carbon—the basic stuff of life on the planet, the perfect fuel—and just a dash of air, and you have light in abundance. It's all in what you need at the time.

Fire draws us like friendship. It fascinates us from our earliest experiences with its lovely light. It is beautiful and dangerous, seductive and comforting, frightening and useful. Of what else could we ask so much?

Blue flame, comet sparks, glowing tanager embers, and a fire enveloping heat. I am defined by the campfire and the night. My boundaries are discovered in firelight. I feel my own skin luxuriantly; I am aware of every inch of it as it is turned to the light, warmed, expanded slightly like bread dough rising in the warmth; turned away from the light, I feel constricted, chill, shrunken—a minor winter. Heat and light explore my face intermittently as the campfire flares; my cheeks feel the touch, and my eyelids, kissed by fire. My hair is smoke scented, my skin is burnished with it. I am defined by fire.

I nudge a log with my toe to better position it, and it flares as bright as memory; fire is an invitation to time travel, as well. Add this to its attributes. I am as present as ever Ram Dass could have wished; I am here, now. But as I stare into this small fire before me, in a specific place on the planet—it could scarcely be more specific!—in the northwest quadrant of Missouri on this mellow September night, I see into the past without my bidding it.

I am seven and lying beside a fire on an Ozark summer sandbar, watching the logs turn to ashes through sleepy lids, fingers and cheeks still sticky with webs of melted marshmallow. The sand curves to fit my curveless child's body, and I curl, content, in the old down bag that smells permanently of canvas and camphor and woodsmoke. The firelight catches the long silver of our canoe, plating it with copper, and touches the tops of the quick, shining riffles with blaze orange.

My father fishes nearby; I hear the liquid plop as his lure hits the water, the whir of his reel like a gigantic mosquito when he draws it back. I see his knotty arms in the firelight as if they were carved from burl maple, and I am as safe as ever I've been under childhood's covers. I don't care if we ever leave the circle of firelight that holds the strange night at a comfortable distance; I am deliciously and blindly at peace. I taste my still-sweet lips, sugared with marshmallow, and drift off to sleep in wildness. ❧

THE IMMENSITY OF SKY

Gretel Ehrlich left a frenzied but highly productive filmmaking career in New York for the wide-open spaces of Wyoming during the dying process of the man she loved. The comforts of familiar neighborhood and old friends had failed her, and comfort itself had come to seem only a disguise for discomfort.

The immensity of space out in Wyoming is so overwhelming and expansive that for those who have not experienced it, it is difficult to imagine. Few have captured its windy, harsh, and dramatic beauty as well as Ehrlich. She writes: "The truest art I would strive for in any work would be to give the page the same qualities as earth: weather would land on it harshly; light would elucidate the most difficult truths; wind would sweep away obtuse padding. Finally, the lessons of impermanence taught me this: loss constitutes an odd kind of fullness; despair empties out into an unquenchable appetite for life." As friends demanded to know when she was going to "quit hiding out" in Wyoming, she was discovering something larger, something truer and simpler in the hard physical work of sheep ranching. Wyoming's is a topography that rises up bucking, shaking off any words that attempt to attach themselves to it. —S. Z.

Excerpts from *The Solace of Open Spaces* by

GRETEL EHRLICH

It's May and I've just awakened from a nap, curled against sagebrush the way my dog taught me to sleep—sheltered from wind. A front is pulling the huge sky over me, and from the dark a hailstone has hit me on the head. I'm trailing a band of two thousand sheep across a stretch of Wyoming badlands, a fifty-mile trip that takes five days because sheep shade up in hot sun and won't budge until it's cool. Bunched together now, and excited into a run by the storm, they drift

41

across dry land, tumbling into draws like water and surge out again onto the rugged, choppy plateaus that are the building blocks of this state.

The name Wyoming comes from an Indian word meaning "at the great plains," but the plains are really valleys, great arid valleys, sixteen hundred square miles, with the horizon bending up on all sides into mountain ranges. This gives the vastness a sheltering look.

Winter lasts six months here. Prevailing winds spill snowdrifts to the east, and new storms from the northwest replenish them. This white bulk is sometimes dizzying, even nauseating, to look at. At twenty, thirty, and forty degrees below zero, not only does your car not work, but neither do your mind and body. The landscape hardens into a dungeon of space. During the winter, while I was riding to find a new calf, my jeans froze to the saddle, and in the silence that such cold creates I felt like the first person on earth, or the last.

Today the sun is out—only a few clouds billowing. In the east, where the sheep have started off without me, the benchland tilts up in a series of eroded red-earthed mesas, planed flat on top by a million years of water; behind them, a bold line of muscular scarps rears up ten thousand feet to become the Big Horn Mountains. A tidal pattern is engraved into the ground, as if left by the sea that once covered this state. Canyons curve down like galaxies to meet the oncoming rush of flat land.

To live and work in this kind of open country, with its hundred-mile views, is to lose the distinction between background and foreground. When I asked an older ranch hand to describe Wyoming's openness, he said, "It's all a bunch of nothing—wind and rattlesnakes—and so much of it you can't tell where you're going or where you've been and it don't make much difference." John, a sheepman I know, is tall and handsome and has an explosive temperament. He has a perfect intuition about people and sheep. They call him "Highpockets," because he's so long-legged; his graceful stride matches the distance he has to cover. He says, "Open space hasn't affected me at all. It's all the people moving in on it." The huge ranch he was born on takes up much of one county and spreads into another state; to put 100,000 miles on his pickup in three years and never leave home is not unusual. A friend of mine has an aunt who ranched on Powder River and didn't go off her place for eleven years. When her husband died, she quickly moved to town, bought a car, and drove around the States to see what she'd been missing.

Most people tell me they've simply driven through Wyoming, as if there were nothing to stop for. Or else they've skied in Jackson Hole, a place Wyomingites acknowledge uncomfortably because its green beauty and chic affluence are mismatched with the rest of the state. Most of Wyoming has a "lean-to" look. Instead of big, roomy barns and Victorian houses, there are dugouts, low sheds, log cabins, sheep camps, and fence lines that look like driftwood blown haphazardly into place. People here still feel pride because they live in such a harsh place, part of the glamorous cowboy past, and they are determined not to be the victims of a mining-dominated future.

Most characteristic of the state's landscape is what a developer euphemistically describes as "indigenous growth right up to your front door"—a reference to waterless stands of salt sage, snakes, jack rabbits, deerflies, red dust, a brief respite of wildflowers, dry washes, and no trees. In the Great Plains the vistas look like music, like Kyries of grass, but Wyoming seems to be the doing of a mad architect—tumbled and twisted, ribboned with faded, deathbed colors, thrust up and pulled down as if the place had been startled out of a deep sleep and thrown into a pure light.

I came here four years ago. I had not planned to stay, but I couldn't make myself leave. John, the sheepman, put me to work immediately. It was spring, and shearing time. For fourteen days of fourteen hours each, we moved thousands of sheep through sorting corrals to be sheared, branded, and deloused. I suspect that my original motive for coming here was to "lose myself" in new and unpopulated territory. Instead of producing the numbness I thought I wanted, life on the sheep ranch woke me up. The vitality of the people I was working with flushed out what had become a hallucinatory rawness inside me. I threw away my clothes and bought new ones; I cut my hair. The arid country was a clean slate. Its absolute indifference steadied me.

Sagebrush covers 58,000 square miles of Wyoming. The biggest city has a population of fifty thousand, and there are only five settlements that could be called cities in the whole state. The rest are towns, scattered across the expanse with as much as sixty miles between them, their populations two thousand, fifty, or ten. They are fugitive-looking, perched on a barren, windblown bench, or tagged onto a river or a railroad, or laid out straight in a farming valley with implement stores and a block-long Mormon church. In the eastern part of the state, which slides down into the Great Plains, the new mining settlements are boomtowns, trailer cities, metal knots on flat land.

Despite the desolate look, there's a coziness to living in this state. There are so few people (only 470,000) that ranchers who buy and sell cattle know one another statewide; the kids who choose to go to college usually go to the state's one university, in Laramie; hired hands work their way around Wyoming in a lifetime of hirings and firings. And despite the physical separation, people stay in touch, often driving two or three hours to another ranch for dinner.

Seventy-five years ago, when travel was by buckboard or horseback, cowboys who were temporarily out of work rode the grub line—drifting from ranch to ranch, mending fences or milking cows, and receiving in exchange a bed and meals. Gossip and messages traveled this slow circuit with them, creating an intimacy between ranchers who were three and four weeks' ride apart. One old-time couple I know, whose turn-of-the-century homestead was used by an outlaw gang as a relay station for stolen horses, recall that if you were traveling, desperado or not, any lighted ranch house was a welcome sign. Even now, for someone who lives in a remote spot, arriving at a ranch or coming to town for supplies is cause for celebration. To emerge from isolation can be disorienting. Everything looks bright, new vivid. After I had been herding sheep for only three days, the sound of the camp tender's pickup flustered me. Longing for human company, I felt a foolish grin take over my face; yet I had to resist an urgent temptation to run and hide. ✳

OF CARIBOU AND SNOWY PLACES

Margaret E. Murie, born in 1902, grew up in Seattle, Washington, in a household that welcomed expeditions into the out-of-doors. The same year that she was the first woman graduate of the new University of Alaska, she married Olaus Murie, a wildlife biologist doing research in Alaska. They honeymooned in Alaska's backcountry, a daunting trek for a lesser woman but one that became a great and wonderful adventure for Murie. Enjoying her new husband's pleasure in nature, she recognized over time the necessity of wilderness in her own life. She and her husband went on to play important roles in the founding and leadership of the Wilderness Society

Much of Two in the Far North, *the book from which this excerpt is taken, is in the form of ebullient diary entries which record her detailed observations and an intimacy with nature that paralleled the developing intimacy of her new marriage. Murie's writing has also become an important historic record of the Alaska of the early 1920s. Battling mosquitoes, isolation, and equipment problems, Murie's writing continually blossoms with a celebration of wilderness that reflects her joy in life and in "being out." She is a wise woman of courage and humor whose readers will adore following her outdoors. —A. Z.*

Excerpts from *Two in the Far North* by

MARGARET E. MURIE

For six weeks Olaus and I had been apart for only a few hours now and then. The last two days of October it was all different. The three caribou hides had to be dried for shipment. They were hung on a rope stretched inside the ridgepole from one end of the tent to the other, and for those two days I stayed there to keep the fire going in the tiny stove to dry the hides, while Olaus hunted more caribou atop the mountain across the river. Imagine an eight-by-ten tent occupied by three caribou hides, including hoofs, various camp equipment, one girl, no reading matter, and you have the picture. I was learning a bit more about being married to a scientist.

Why had I been so zealous in paring down our load at Wiseman? Here I was without a magazine or a book; the little Dunsany book could just as well have been put in. Oh well, at least there was some enjoyment in knowing how the many lone trappers and miners in that north country must feel. All my life I had heard stories about their having nothing to do but read the labels on cans. That second day I read every label in the grub bag. The milk cans were especially nice; they had recipes on them. I looked them over, but they had all come out of the same case, I guess, so I memorized the recipe for creamed clams that was on every one of them. Hard to tell when we should ever see a clam! Our ham was wrapped in a page from a magazine, and I shall forever be wondering whether the wandering son got back to the old homestead and his childhood sweetheart before his poor old mother passed away!

Well—time to turn the hides over again. I got used to their odor and didn't mind so much having them dangling over my shoulders whichever way I turned; caribou hides were never so carefully nursed. And I did have the dogs for company, and when too stiff from sitting, I could go out for a few minutes' romp with Ungiak; but soon it was time to crawl back in and stoke the fire again.

·   ·   ·

Climbing a mountain on snowshoes is an entirely different affair from flip-flopping over the tundra on them. It was such a release to be out of the tent and going along again, such fun crossing the river, with Ungiak running circles around us in jubilation at being allowed to go along too. But by the time we were halfway up the mountain I was puffing outrageously, and had fallen down and painfully untangled myself seven times while Ungiak helpfully stepped all over me and the snowshoes. I had also lost a lot of breath just laughing, and my throat seemed sealed and dry. Visions of frosty lemonades and ice cream sodas floated irrepressibly through my mind.

Ungiak and I were finally left to sit on a hummock and eat snow while Olaus sped on up to the summit, seemingly as effortlessly as a caribou. Could I ever achieve that physical efficiency? I suddenly seemed to hear dear old Jim Hagan's voice back in Fairbanks that previous winter: "You go ahead and marry that fellow; he's a fine one. The only thing is, I don't know how you're ever going to keep up with him. He's half caribou, you know."

·   ·   ·

We were traveling south on an overland route, jogging along over the best trail we had had so far. I could ride on the runners at the handle bars most of the way, and often Olaus left the gee pole and sat on the load up front while we talked over the past weeks, which would light our lives forever.

An uphill start is no cause for rejoicing on any day, for the morning enthusiasm of the dogs is too soon spent. This morning we were winded the first hundred feet; all our limbs ached; the fatigue poisons were still present. Yet up and still up the trail went, rough and sidling, so that it took all my weight on the handle bars and Olaus's against the gee pole to keep the heavy sled from sliding off against stumps. This continued for what seemed hours, upgrade for three miles.

The descent on the other side was worse. Stubs and bumps and hummocks dotted the middle of the barely snowed-over trail; the dogs went faster and faster, Olaus hopping over obstructions and trying to hold back on the gee pole, while I stood with both feet on the brake, accomplishing nothing. The brake kept bouncing over the bumps until the soles of my feet were aching. Olaus shouted back: "Don't try to; it doesn't do any good anyway." So we went drunkenly on to the bottom and straight going again.

Straight going did not mean smooth going. No attempt was made to smooth over the surface when an Alaskan mail trail was slashed through the forest. Before sufficient snow falls, willow stubs, small stumps, tussocks, hummocks, and bumps have to be negotiated as best one can. We had a load of five hundred pounds with only seven dogs, and a fourteen-foot sled to manage. The mailman was required to carry no more than two hundred pounds of mail on this route. Even at that, I will still swear that all Alaskan mail carriers of that era were heroes.

From the diary:

November 16: . . . The trail is much better, with more snow, but the way to Tanana seems to be up hill, down dale, all the way. Sometimes we cross a broad white expanse of lake dotted with black muskrat houses, sometimes we follow a winding slough with yellow grass still standing above the snow and exquisite silvery birches frosty on knolls above it; then up another wooded hill through spruces getting larger as we travel south. These are beautiful hills, and always from the tops there are views which lift the spirit and make the long climbs worthwhile. Southward we gaze on terraced slopes, splashed with crystal-shining birches and magenta-hued willows, dropping gently away to a stream valley far below; beyond that more wooded slopes and the pink and snowy peaks of the Beaver Mountains far over on the Great River.

On our fourth day south we caught up with a part of that same caribou herd which on its southward migration had caused such excitement in Wiseman. We were bumping along down a rough slope full of those tussocks again, when old Wolf's ears pricked up and Mayuk, his partner, gave a yelp and in a flash they were all off on a mad run. Over on the next slope we saw twelve or fifteen buff-brown caribou, and on slopes further off, more and more. One small band was feeding along close to the trail ahead, and the Victoria Land hunters were straining every muscle to reach them. There was nothing we could do but hang on to the sled and pray it wouldn't tip over. . . .

November 18: So short are the days becoming that the fiery glory of the red sunrise seems almost to merge into the delicate rosy saffron glow of sunset, so that we travel across a colorful stage setting and watch green spruces, red willows, snowy birches, undergo strange and delightful changes of color. Out across the snow-covered tundra a snowy owl sits calm and inscrutable on a birch stub, the startling, beautiful ghost of the Arctic. Behind his whiteness the western sky is shell-pink. Words can never tell the peace, the strength, the triumphant beauty of this land.

Then very soon the sky is midnight blue and fully spangled with stars, and the moon is rising brighter and brighter behind the pointed trees. In the north a flicker of green and yellow; then an unfurled bolt of rainbow ribbon shivering and shimmering across the stars—the Aurora. The dogs begin to speed up; we must be nearing a cabin; yes, there it is, a little black blotch on the creek bank. The air is cold and tingling, fingers are numb. A great dark form flops slowly across the trail—a great horned owl, the speaking spirit of the wilderness.

November 19: We had traveled five hours before daybreak; hours of misty moonlight in an unreal quiet white world. In silence we were sliding out of our beloved North. The dogs padded softly along, slowly, steadily, up a long hill, through black silent forest, and out upon a bare summit.

Standing close together at the handle bars, we looked to the south. Below us wooded terraces descended to the Yukon. The river was a glimmering expanse in the faint light of a gold horizon glowing brighter each moment. Looming against the yellow sky, above the smokes of Tanana, the great granite promontory where the Tanana, a smooth white avenue, merged with that greater white ribbon, the Yukon. There lay our road to civilization.

But we turned away from all that, turned back north the way we had come—looked down into the white valley we had just traversed. And through our minds ran the picture of all those other valleys beyond, of rivers bordered with woods, grassy sloughs, wide white lakes, on and on to the white Endicott peaks—to that happy valley of the Koyukuk, the river of golden autumn, golden dreams, and brave laughing souls. While our hearts went winging back over those miles, and our tears brimmed over, our feet had to turn south.

"All right, Pooto!" And the sturdy dog feet padded swiftly on toward the sunrise—once more a rosy sunrise over the willows of the Yukon. ❧

ON THE EDGE

Gabrielle Daniels's first contact with the wild came on the edge of an island forest at the Hedgebrook Cottages for Women Writers in Washington state. It was a contact as frightening as it was illuminating to her inner-city eyes. Woods around the cottages stretch darkly back; one winds through their tunnels as blackberry and other shrubs grasp at one's clothes, birds chirrup, and animals scratch. Approaching in solitude, unsettled and cautious at first, Daniels faces her fears and then embraces her own wild origins. Unspoken but present throughout this excerpt is Daniels's lasting terror after an attempted rape several years before her wilderness sojourn.

Daniels, a resident of San Francisco, California, used the forest setting for a longer essay from which this excerpt is taken, searching back through her African roots, her African-American ancestry, and into her personal contemporary urban angst. Although I am a naturalist and have been for a long time, Daniels's experience of wilderness, the freshness of her perspective, enlivened my own. —S. Z.

Excerpts from *A City Girl Discovers the Forest* by

GABRIELLE DANIELS

It's usually early afternoon when I take a walk. Today I've been up since about eight and writing since nine-thirty. I've eaten lunch and I want the meal to circulate in my body rather than sit like stones slowly melting in my stomach during a siesta. I slide into my don't-stop green Sportos, take up the walking stick leaning near the door, and head up the trails.

There's a semblance of wilderness around Hedgebrook Farm, a women writers' colony that's my home for two months. Grasses and secondary growth encroach, seemingly waiting for their chance. Trails wind around the six cottages and the farmhouse where we meet for dinner and activities, and then continue into the woods. Some of the trails are large enough for a small truck to pass through, some are simple footpaths. I am fascinated by the little heaps of stone which appear here and there, unsure whether they are pointing out a new path. I wonder how much farther my path will go.

I feel like a deer. I can't believe that the quiet is safe. Sunlight peers through the trees. I lean on my third leg, the piebald walking stick. Hearing tree frogs call to each other, I am startled. I strain my ears for an enemy that never appears. A yellowed leaf spirals and flutters to my feet like Mary Poppins' umbrella.

Spider webs flatten against my face like veils. I take off my glasses, dry wipe my face, dust my hair for creepy crawlies, and brush my shoulders. A dragonfly takes dead aim for my chest and lands. It's been a long time since I've had this kind of attention; I frantically shoo it away. When I was a child, my friends and I called them mosquito hawks. They fed on mosquitoes, carriers of diseases that existed long before we were born, diseases like yellow fever and vomito, the New Orleans scourge. Seeing a mosquito hawk is a pleasure; they have disappeared even from the open spaces in the suburbs, like the doodlebugs and ladybugs that we'd let crawl all over our hands. Only certain insects have survived in the cities. Flies. Ants. Moths. Cockroaches, the most hardy. Mostly scavengers. Pests. We'd watch caterpillars munching on poinsettias, sucking their milk, and green lizards and, if we were lucky, small snakes. We wished for a real hurricane, so the levees would "bust" and we'd really see the moccasins we'd been told about, or even a gator. The mosquito hawk gets the message: it has dropped down on some tetchy animal—me. It flies high, takes a ninety degree turn toward the berry patch, and disappears.

Mushrooms have sprouted everywhere since the rain, many sizes, shapes, and colors. A gigantic white mushroom looms from under some brush. It must be a toadstool, but it is as big as a child's wagon wheel, with a thick stem. Big enough for Holly, our house manager, to brew several bowls of soup, if it is not poisonous. Several mushroom patches are already turning brown, fading back into the dead soil, ready for another episode of rain. It's like playing hopscotch, studying the ground, self-consciously avoiding where they grow. Where I least expect it, I nearly mash one growing defiantly purple and bumpy and alone in the middle of the trail.

There's been some logging and clearing of firewood for the cottage dwellers; little caches are curing, stacked in the open and covered with plastic. During the storms some trees have blown down or are on their way to the ground. They lean as if defying gravity, hoping that something like a nearby tree will break their fall: Catch her, catch her! Dead trees wear little orange ties about them as if dressed nattily for death, though their roots still cling tenaciously to the soil. Some look naked and sad, their stark boughs reaching out in the air: why, why? The stumps are another story—happy, teeming condominiums. If it isn't lichen spreading on the stump, it's insects chewing through the bark, weeds choking the roots.

The trail, strewn with fading wet leaves and fallen branches, crunches or slides under my feet. The sound scares off a blue heron, the first I've ever seen in the wild, which spreads its magnificent wings and alights on a nearby bough, watching me. I sit on a rock beside Green Pond. Unlike a man-made waterfall and its pond, this pool doesn't drain off. It is very still and black as yin with a burgeoning coverlet of algae, leaves, pollen and some kind of bog clover. The heron gazes, disapprovingly I think, over his shoulder at me. He wants me to leave. This is his pond. I am his predator and I could hurt him. He will not come down closer to me. He will groom himself and wait for me to leave. I watch the stillness of the pond, the reflection of the trees framing it. A camera snapshot would not do justice to this picture in my mind. The air is fresh; I breathe in and the trees breathe out, the lungs of the earth.

How can you leave your cottage, your car unlocked, the windows wide open and challenging? I tried it once or twice until my thoughts hyperventilated. I worry because I have always lived in the city. I am a person who scratches her driver's license number on what little she possesses, who was robbed while a student, who leaves the lights blazing and the TV talking when I am gone at night.

It is dark around four in the afternoon, as October has somersaulted into November as gently as scattering leaves. Less than a month to go at this writing retreat. A storm is buffeting the island, but it is mostly wind; the rain hasn't yet arrived. The trees are swaying with a whoom, whoom! I sweep the flashlight in a protective arc every few paces. Everything is rustling, twisting and bowing. The wind parts my unbuttoned coat like a knee between my legs; it flaps. I look up. The darkness reveals not trees but boughs like shadowy, many-headed hydras. They could fall on me, their fantastic weight crushing me flat, to death. I feel like running, but if I run, I'll panic. . . . I take a deep breath as the wind swallows my face, whips my hair.

Sometimes I think black people forget that we were once an agrarian people, that we lived most of our lives, seventy-five or eighty years, on the land. That our most vivid cultural memories, even from the time before slavery, spring from our connection to this land. That we celebrated the harvest and believed in our own hands. That we joined with the other original people, the Native Americans, whose respect for the land mirrored our own. Runago, runago. That we have always fought for our claim to this land, through hunger and debt. That while we continued on the land, the spirits continued to live with us and within us.

And yet we try in the cities. The Fillmore District, where I spent my first two years in California, is now in the last stages of "redevelopment" and is almost unrecognizable to me. Here, at the age of seven, I fell in love with real quarter-pound burgers and the busy, jooking bars. I saw the Ice Capades at the Winterland before the hippies flocked to concerts there. Today, the remaining black citizens, mostly elderly, fight in vain to keep the community gardens in two colorful blocks, gardens incongruous with the surrounding high-rises and condos marching from Pacific Heights.

I am in the boonies, I tell myself. I have no health care until I return to work at Stanford in mid-December, stay well! Suddenly I don't want to go back to the cottage, not just yet. I don't need a bus. Get your walking stick, I think, let's go to Green Pond, I've never seen it in the rain.

In taking those small steps, I see the forest for the first time. Before, whenever I'd leave the forest, I always felt as if I had missed or overlooked something. There was too much to take in at one time, waves of information to my senses seemed jumbled and sometimes unfriendly. I wonder whether I'd been hurrying through, identifying sights as if they were separate from the habitat. Now, I am overcome. I look up and around me. The trees are heavy with moisture, their canopies gaze down quietly, their trunks stand like the bare legs of grownups. Except for the downpour, the only sound is the croak of a tree frog hidden in a tangle.

I've been looking for Hedgebrook's spirit tree. I've been drawn to the spirit tree's cousins—the pieces of trees I've burned, the kind with bumps, knots and hollows and twists, with dead lichen, with strange hieroglyphs where the bark separates from the wood. They are different, interesting. At home, I purposely buy deformed vegetables in the supermarket. I think it's magical to eat something so imperfect from a processed world. A gift.

I want to stand under the twisted magic of that tree and hear only the wind. And I want to remember another night when, in a vision, a bear crashed out of the woods and gently licked the sole of my foot and then turned and went away, dragging all the woods—twigs, leaves, horns, sap mixed with defecation and feathers—stuck to its furry backside. I felt the tingles on my right foot even days later.

The forest is only what we choose to see out of our fears and myths. Most of the time it is dim and unknown. We hear the keening of hawks and eagles, the buzzing of cicadas mating, and we think there is danger. We attack without reason. When it is chopped or scythed down, when it is finally prone and overcome and cleared, there is nothing left but rotting stumps, space, and dead leaves scattering on the wind. Generations are cut off, heredity and possibility for difference and change stand still for the sake of control. And where was the monster after all? Where does it reside? Did it ever live among these boughs, these leaves? And the axes are turned in yet another direction. There, and there, and there. The endlessness, the open-mouthed voraciousness of the chase to subdue. Between court orders, let them sneak in and cut and haul the beautiful ones away. Despite periodic complaints, let the train of tank cars full of chemicals fall into the river, choking the fish, turning the clear blue waters a smoky green, mocking us.

Unlike Sojourner Truth, the forest is forcibly trained. Like bad nappy hair it is processed into good straight hair until one tree looks like another. Every tree, like every black woman, is different, full of intimate magic. We dare to name ourselves. Cypress, redwood, sycamore, chestnut, yucca, willow. Eartha, Andrewnetta, Oletha, Syrtiller, Mattiwilda. ❧

BOUNDED BY SEA

Jan DeBlieu writes about the discovery of home on the Outer Banks, that wild rim of islands in the Atlantic that protect the inner shore. DeBlieu's background is journalism and she has frequently written about the natural world and the problems that beset it. This passage is more personal, extracted from Hatteras Journal, *her book which records life there from the measured daily rhythm of her beach walks to the frightening interruption of a hurricane.*

DeBlieu exemplifies one of the rewards of becoming conversant with the place where you live: a freshened knowledge of what else lives there and how they go about their business of living, a growing and satisfying connection with wilderness. In exploring the open beaches, she became entranced with the comings and goings of the natural world about her, from the microscopic creatures that live between sand grains to the whales that pass by the coast. As a woman and as a writer she shares her pleasure in the landscape with us, her delight in research and in learning about dunes and crabs and oat grass and the whole panoply of littoral life. In doing so she delineates her connectedness with the natural world, her own necessity of wilderness. —A. Z.

Excerpts from *Hatteras Journal* by

JAN DeBLIEU

Just after dawn on a cloudless mid-May morning, I hiked north on the beach to a set of tall, crumbling dunes. There is a southwest wind, still gaining force, that catches foam and occasionally hurls it back over the shoulders of a breaker the way a woman might toss a long braid. The beach's pitch is steep; to find the most level walking I stay on high sand, away from the line of tides. A bank of fog hovers on the eastern horizon and—for the fourth straight morning—obscures the sun's emergence from the sea. I have yet to see a true sunrise on Hatteras. By noon the fog will have burned off, but I would lay money down that at daybreak it will be back.

I walk this stretch often in first light, which in May sneaks across the island between 5:30

and 6:00. Twenty-five miles east of the mainland, in a landscape of white sand and glare, the term "early" takes on particularly harsh meaning. By 6:15 bright yellow sunshine slips through curtains and floods under doors. By 6:30 a good portion of the island population is up, dressed, and well into their work. To me it is worth the pain of rising in the dark to be out for the early morning light. Just past sunrise it strikes the Hatteras sand with a gilding intensity that is lost as the sun ascends. For a few minutes the reeds and grasses take on an orange sheen that makes it seem as if they are lit from within, like a candle or a Japanese lamp. . . .

Morning is my favorite time here, but it is not the only time I come. The panorama from the top of the dunes is always impressive, if only for its limitless scope. Neither trees nor buildings block my horizons; in any direction I can see to the curve of the earth. Half of my view is taken up by a sky that deepens in blue at its top and thins almost to white at its edges, the other half by water and a narrow, undulating strip of sand. There are no cozy thickets in sight, no protected coves. No oil rigs mar the eastern horizon; no mainland hovers on the west to anchor Hatteras to the rest of the world.

I could sit here all day, twirling sea oats around my fingers and burying my feet in cool sand; just sit and think about landscapes, seascapes, and the psychological consequences of living where the two collide. Between boundless horizons my own possibilities seem boundless, and my most pressing problems wither in size. I once read that many primitive cultures associate wide spaces with freedom and adventure, while forests, valleys, and sheltered coves evoke feelings of security and warmth. If so, it makes sense that the first people to come here were intrepid souls looking for a place where they could live unencumbered by traditional law.

A sense of freedom abounds, but at the sacrifice of comfort. For all practical purposes I am sitting in the middle of a desert. Nothing flourishes here that needs much fresh water, or that lacks hardiness and the determination to survive. You cannot escape the salt, the sun, the rotten-egg stench of marsh, the mosquitoes and greenhead flies. The coast is not a place where you can easily ignore the elements. Storms can be seen for miles advancing like spreading stains. The sea sloshes dark and broody beneath a pastel dawn, or flaccid and green below thunderheads. The wind, when it cannot be felt or heard, imposes its presence by jostling bushes and whipping whitecaps on the sound. And yet the clearness of the light, the constant swish of the surf, and the yield of the sand underfoot spark a sensuousness that strips aside the discomfort I would normally feel in such a barren and hostile setting.

Each element—earth, wind, water—wields a double-edged sword of pleasure and pain. The sand that molds itself so comfortably around your feet and body becomes, in high wind, a brutal, solid sleet. A heavy breeze steals your breath, but a light one whistles through your nostrils and virtually does your breathing for you. The surf can chill you with its violence, or it can lick the beach in a soothing, two-count rhythm. I walk on the beach to relax. . . .

Late in April the beach at Rodanthe began to fill with holes I knew to be the entrances to ghost crab burrows. Anyone who has spent time on the middle and southern Atlantic coast has seen these sandy shelled crabs that retreat to underground chambers in the hottest part of the day. Long thought to be scavengers—the garbage collectors who clean the beaches of dead organisms—ghost crabs are really adept predators who feed on mole crabs and coquinas. Field guides frequently describe them as an evolutionary link between animals of the land and the sea, since they cannot swim but must wet their gills with ocean water at least once a day. Their genus name, *Ocypode*, derives from a Greek phrase meaning swift-footed. This seems especially appropriate for a crab that can run as quickly as five feet a second. Their most engaging feature is well-developed eyes, which protrude a half-inch above their shells on shiny black stalks. . . .

Quietly I mounted a steep dune and peered over the top. On the beach thirty-odd ghost crabs busied themselves with pushing sand from the entrances to their burrows and skittering back and forth to the surf. They ran sideways on butter-colored legs with their ivory claws in front of them, tips down. Most of them glided across the sand in a straight path to and from the sea, but a few moved in short bursts toward the north or south, darting in and out of holes. At the sight of me they froze with their eyes turned in my direction.

I topped the dune and crouched in full view of the crabs. The sand was littered with chunks of cocoa-brown peat, cracked and crusty from the sun. From behind several of these, eye stalks protruded like periscopes. I kept still despite a twinge of uneasiness; when I looked to the left, I was painfully aware of the beady eyes that studied me from the right. After three or four minutes a few crabs turned back to slinging sand from the burrows. Others resumed their dancing to the surf. I lowered myself slowly from a crouch to a sitting position.

Suddenly on the fringe of the colony two large crabs ran toward each other, raised high on sinewy legs, and rammed together. They pushed hard against each other with their claws for twenty seconds before one lowered itself, folding its legs beneath it, and backed away. The victor advanced aggressively on tiptoe, its claws pushed out, as a half-dozen crabs peeked from burrows or blocks of peat. The losing crab continued to inch away, nearly flattening itself against the sand. A quick movement at the edge of the colony caught my eye. Another two of the largest crabs collided and pushed with what appeared to be all their might, stepping sideways for balance, flailing their legs. They separated after perhaps ten seconds, waving their claws at each other the way an angry man might shake his fist, and parted.

Around me more shoving matches began. . . . The matches were sporadic and usually ended with no clear victor. In the background the surf pummeled the beach, its roar the morning's only sound. A large orange sun backlit the crabs, shining through their brittle legs and giving their silent antics the quality of the surreal. . . .

The sun's glare was growing painful, and my sunglasses were in the truck. I stood up as slowly as I could. Three dozen ghost crabs froze. See you later fellows, I thought. Maybe same time tomorrow. ❧

SPIRIT SONG

Robin Tekwelus Youngblood describes herself as a bridge between ancient European traditions and those of several Native nations. Her Okanagan/San Poil ancestors roamed the Okanagan valley from Kamloops, in what is now Canada, to the Columbia River in north-central Washington. Youngblood's Cherokee forebears walked the Trail of Tears from North Carolina to Oklahoma during the years 1839 through 1842. Researching her French, Irish, and Welsh ancestry has given her insight into the uncanny parallels between Druidic and Native American earth-based beliefs.

Youngblood is the mother of a daughter and son and the grandmother of four. She has grounded her children in such Native traditions as the Sun Dance ways of the Lakota Sioux and the Winter Dance ceremonial of the Okanagan. An artist in three disciplines, she paints and creates shields, drums, and rattles; leads ceremonies; and writes prose and poetry. She plans a pilgrimage to North Carolina to meet her Cherokee relatives and is currently writing a novel based on the Okanagan people stretching back to pre-European contact.

This essay is set on land, the lower half of which she owns, abutting the high country of the Okanagan National Forest. Although this inward and outward journey could be called a "vision quest," its simple, direct and profound connection with wilderness is accessible to all of us. —S. Z.

The Place of My Ancestors by
ROBIN TEKWELUS YOUNGBLOOD

I remember mother telling me to look for the faces of my ancestors in the clouds. Today they are in a rush, scudding by like ponies with long white manes racing for the horizon. In the upper ether the wind is raging, although it barely whispers where I sit. In this stillness I answer to no one except those who preceded me.

The land beneath my feet tugs at me, as roots to a tree. This place resides somewhere deep in my DNA. It must, because I didn't even know my connection to it the first time I came here. It called me, and called again, until finally I answered its pull.

I descend from the Okanagan/San Poil, among other peoples, and this rich mountain soil feels like home to me. Reaching down, I scoop a handful of loose, humus-enriched earth and hold it beneath my nose. It is fragrant with the lifetimes of ancient forests. I can almost smell the deer that trod here five hundred years ago, the sage grouse who nested here in the last century, and the mole who burrowed into his den at this point just a week past. As I walk the trail, touching the giant tamaracks and Douglas Fir, I see those-who-have-gone-before-me walking this way. The silken grasses in the high prairie below me undulate like the coat of a buffalo ruffled by the breeze.

Later this afternoon, the wind will sing through the trees as it soughs its way down the canyon. I know this from experience; it's happened every day of every stay. I count on it. My drum, rattle, flute, and I will accompany it on its journey to the ancient one's ears. This is my give-away to those who once lived in the heart of this country. I will sing the old songs that the mountain has given me—songs of the flicker, the deer, and sister golden hair, Mel Keep Oops, the prairie eagle. I will sing the new songs that my brothers and sisters from the powwows and the Sun and Corn dances have given me, for they too carry power and will give vitality to the living history of this mountain.

Though I love this place, I always feel an ache of sorrow as I tread these mountain paths. This moss, the lichen, bitterroot, camas, elk and deer, and the trout in the streams were all honored deeply and shared freely among a great people who today barely exist on a few thousand of the millions of acres they once roamed. Only a few miles away there will soon be a gold mine leaching cyanide into the underground water tables. Already many of the hills below have been clear cut. The fish dwindle in the mountain lakes. The Okanagan no longer sees the salmon, for the Columbia has been damned— and so have our people. In my own way I am reclaiming this valley, these strong and towering mountains, for my people. I will do the ceremonies to bring them back. I will take in the joy of this place and send its light to those I love.

As twilight descended last night, a long-eared owl glided without a sound past my campfire. The coyotes barked and howled as they traversed the valley on their nocturnal hunt. Listening to the pattern of their calls just as I was dropping off to sleep, I imagined one flushing a rabbit from some den on the far side of the small arroyo below me, signaling to others on my side who would close the circle around the hare, until Mr. Rabbit became nothing but food for thought.

This morning at dawn, my dog Wotai, which means "sacred token" in Sioux, awakened me with a low growl. I heard a sort of snuffling noise outside the tent, and peeking out saw myself surrounded by thirty-two elk grazing the mountain meadow. They were aware of my presence but evidently sensed no danger. They were at peace, enjoying their breakfast, basking in shafts of sunshine. I munched a piece of pemmican in silent tribute to their willingness to share their territory with me. Such graceful beauty! An elegant, powerful and stately bull turned towards me, rack held proudly aloft, and gazed directly into my eyes. I felt a thrill; in some intangible way our spirits communicated. I heard again my grandmother's stories of how the animals once talked with people.

Wotai, my half-Husky friend, has been my constant companion ever since he came to me with all the adoration his six weeks of life could express. He and I sat in the tent most of this morning. He needed to perform his morning ablutions as I did, but he sensed the importance of this occasion and waited quietly, gently thumping his tail when I looked at him. I knew if either of us moved we'd spook 'their majesties.' I could not disrupt the herd's morning routine. After all, we were guests in their home.

Once all the peoples of the earth knew and understood the importance of living with the land and its creatures instead of dominating them. In this age of industry and technology we have all but forgotten this. Even my people litter powwow grounds, argue over whether or not they should take governmental monies and allow nuclear waste storage on our reservations (the only refuge we have left). And these days, few seem to know how to tan a hide the old way.

As I attune my heart and steps to the rhythm of the mountain, I think that every person on earth ought to spend several weeks in the wilderness every year. It is a grounding experience, healing and thought-provoking. When you sit at the ancient, untroubled base of a 300-year-old cedar tree, industrial waste is clearly a crime of untold proportions. When you feel the sap flowing through that tree and ask her to share her visions of the country she has overseen for centuries, cities are immaterial. As one lays upon the breast of the Mother, counting a profusion of diminutive wildflowers, corporate greed is the penultimate fallacy. What is the dream and what the reality? In its pristine tranquility, I claim this as my reality. Many years ago I developed my own creed: "Do no more damage, and heal what you can."

I feel the heartbeat of my Mother here. These untamed regions speak to me of rootedness, of space and continuity. Wilderness survives, as do we, sometimes precariously and with much needed help; sometimes because she refuses to be overly hospitable to humankind. I often feel the need to protect myself from the roar and tumult of the crowded city, the bigotry and disregard for sacred space that I experience there.

My tipi sets 3,400 feet above the lowlands. It was very interesting the first time we put it up and the rain fell—directly on me! But since then I've learned a little about putting up a tipi, where one should sleep (not in the center!), how to dig the fire pit, and how much wood to use (it's a very small tipi). The frame remains on my land and I take the tent whenever I want to roam.

Tomorrow I go home. Or do I? This is my home, the city is only the place I go to earn a living so that one day I may be able to live here without interruption. There is a humility that I have always sensed in my tribal elders, and when I live in wilderness, a small speck to the great eagle's eye, I know my place. In a strange way, it's comforting, for I see how I fit into the circle of birth, life, death, and rebirth. Here, the hoop is completed and we are all related.

The ancestors smile upon me this morning. I see their faces in the chimerical collection of clouds floating against a pastel sky. A small whirlwind appears beside me. I bow to honor its spirit. A great horned owl sails to a perch in the lodgepole pine near my left shoulder. "Leem Lempt! Coo Koost eeks spoos, eeks Sooh Mee," I say. "Thank you, You have satisfied my heart, my Guardian Spirits." I will return. ❧

THE GUARDIAN

Terry Tempest Williams, a resident of Salt Lake City, is a teacher, a fine naturalist, and a superb ornithologist. She is a young, wise storyteller who combines a love of her native Utah, the richness of her Mormon heritage, and an intimate understanding of the mystical wilderness unfolding about her. She has become an articulate and passionate spokeswoman for all women concerned about the environment. In this age of great haste and pollution and the devourment of Earth's resources, it is women, says Williams, who must be the protectors of the health of the planet and the health of the home. In Refuge, *her best-known book, she bares the terrible truth of death and affirms the incandescence of life.*

In An Unspoken Hunger, *the book of essays from which this excerpt was taken, Williams writes on staying at home, on recording nature where you are as a "radical act." This passage is on Stone Canyon, one of the most charming and evocative canyons on the Colorado River in the Grand Canyon. Williams manages to find time alone, difficult on a crowded commercial river trip, and as readers we tag along on her solitary walk up Stone Canyon, enriched by her intense and immediate affinity with time and place, the splash of gentle water, the magic of maidenhair fern. —A. Z.*

From *An Unspoken Hunger* by

TERRY TEMPEST WILLIAMS

Few know her, but she is always there—Stone Creek Woman—watching over the Colorado River.

Over the years, I have made pilgrimages to her, descending into the Grand Canyon, passing through geologic layers with names like Kayenta, Moenave, Chinle, Shinarump, Toroweep, Coconino, and Supai to guide me down the stone staircase of time. It is always a pleasant journey downriver to Mile 132—Stone Creek, a small tributary that flows into the Colorado. We secure our boats and meander up the side canyon where the heat of the day seeps into our skin, threatens to boil our blood, and we can imagine ourselves as lizards pushing up and down on the hot, coral sand. They watch us step from stone to stone along the streambed. The lizards vanish and then we see her. Stone Creek Woman: guardian of the desert with her redrock face, maidenhair ferns, and waterfall of expression. Moss, the color of emeralds, drapes across her breasts.

I discovered her by accident. My husband, Brooke, and I were with a group on a river trip. It was high noon in June. Twice that morning the boatman had mentioned Stone Creek and what a refuge it would be: the waterfall; the shade-filled canyon; the constant breeze; the deep green pool. Searing heat inspired many of us to jump off the boats before they had been tied down. The group ran up Stone Creek in search of the enchanted pool at the base of the waterfall, leaving me behind.

I sauntered up Stone Creek. Sweat poured off my forehead and I savored the salt on my lips. The dry heat reverberated off the canyon's narrow walls. I relished the sensation of being baked. I walked even more slowly, aware of the cicadas, their drone that held the pulse of the desert. An evening primrose bloomed. I knelt down and peeked inside yellow petals. The pistil and stamens resembled stars. My index finger brushed them, gently, and I inhaled pollen. No act seemed too extravagant in these extreme temperatures. Even the canyon wren's joyous anthem, each falling note, was slow, full, and luxurious. In this heat, nothing was rushed.

Except humans.

Up ahead, I heard laughter, splashing, and the raucous play of friends. I turned the corner and found them bathing, swimming, and sunning. It was a kaleidoscope of color. Lycra bodies, some fat, some thin, sunburned, forgetting all manner of self-consciousness. They were drunk with pleasure.

I sat on a slab of sandstone near the edge of the pool with my knees pulled into my chest and watched, mesmerized by the throbbing waterfall at Stone Creek, its sudden surges of energy, how the moss anchored on the redrock cliff became neon in sunlight, how the long green strands resembled hair, how the fine spray rising from the water nurtured rainbows.

I eventually outwaited everyone. As Brooke led them back to the boats, the glance we exchanged told me I had a few precious moments I could steal for myself. And in that time, I shed my clothing like snakeskin. I swam beneath the waterfall, felt its pelting massage on my back, stood up behind it, turned and touched the moss, the ferns, the slippery rock wall. No place else to be.

I sank into the pool and floated momentarily on my back. The waterfall became my focus once again. Suddenly, I began to see a face emerging from behind the veil of water. Stone Creek Woman. I stood. I listened to her voice.

Since that hot June day, I have made a commitment to visit Stone Creek Woman as often as I can. I believe she monitors the floods and droughts of the Colorado Plateau, and I believe she can remind us that water in the West is never to be taken for granted. When the water flows over the sandstone wall, through the moss and the ferns, she reveals herself. When there is no water, she disappears.

For more than five million years, the Colorado River has been sculpting the Grand Canyon. Stone Creek, as a small tributary to the Colorado, plays its own role in this geologic scheme. The formation I know as Stone Creek Woman has witnessed these changes. The Colorado River, once in the soul-service of cutting through rocks, is now truncated by ten major dams generating twelve million kilowatts of electricity each year. Red water once blessed with sediments from Glen Canyon is now sterile and blue. Cows drink it. We drink it. And crops must be watered. By the time twenty million people in seven western states quench their individual thirsts and hose down two million acres of farmland for their food, the Colorado River barely trickles into the Gulf of California.

If at all.

Water in the American West is blood. Rivers, streams, creeks become arteries, veins, capillaries. Dam, dike, or drain any of them and somewhere, silence prevails. No water: no fish. No water: no plants. No water: no life. Nothing breathes. The land-body becomes a corpse. Stone Creek Woman crumbles and blows away.

Deserts are defined by their dryness, heat, and austerity of form. It is a landscape best described not by what it is, but by what it is not.

It is not green.

It is not lush.

It is not habitable.

Stone Creek Woman knows otherwise. Where there is water, the desert is verdant. Hanging gardens on slickrock walls weep generously with columbines, monkey flowers, and mertensia. A thunderstorm begins to drum. Lightning dances above the mesa. Clouds split. Surging rain scours canyons in a flash of flood. An hour later, there is a clearing. Potholes in the sandstone become basins to drink from. . . .

And here stands Stone Creek Woman, guardian and gauge of the desert, overlooking the Colorado River, with her redrock face, her maidenhair ferns, and waterfall of expression. I have found a handful of people who have seen her. There may be more. Some say she cannot speak. Others will tell you she is only to be imagined. But in the solitude of that side canyon where I swam at her feet, she reminds me we must stand vigilant. Stone Creek Woman begins to dance.

I want to join her. ❧

About the Photographers and the Photographs

KATHY CLAY has traveled widely throughout the United States, capturing America's most spectacular landscapes and wildlands. She has been published in major photographic books including *Streamside Reflections, Bass Fishing, The Rockies, On the Trail of the Desert Wildflower, Seasons of the Coyote, Shadow of the Salmon,* and *Yellowstone: Land of Fire and Ice.* Kathy Clay makes her home in Dubois, Wyoming.

PAGE i—Heath in fall color on Caldera Rim. Yellowstone N.P.

PAGE 28—Sunset light on Sam Rayburn Reservoir. Cassells Boykin S.P.

PAGE 33—Lotus pads backlit with afternoon light. Martin Creek Lake S.P.

PAGE 34—Fall color along Russell Fork River.

PAGE 37—Dew-laden spider web on fall morning. Pipestem S.P.

PAGE 38-39—Fall color, cattails, and mist on Horseshoe Lake.

PAGE 46—Fall colored aspens. Yellowstone N.P.

PAGE 47—Cattails in fall at Rainy Lake. Yellowstone N.P.

PAGE 62—Maple in fall color. Dix Mountain Wilderness.

PAGE 67—Ironwood tree bark.

PAGE 69—Evening light on moss-covered forest floor. Cabwaylingo S.F.

PAGE 71—Cypress, tupelo, and lily pads. Caddo Lake S.P.

PAGE 72—Sunset light on beach. Sea Rim S.P.

PAGE 92—Slot canyon.

KATHLEEN NORRIS COOK is well known for her outstanding images of outdoor subjects, primarily of the western United States. For three consecutive years her work has been selected for display in Kodak's prestigious Professional Photographer's Showcase in the Epcot Center Pavilion. A winner of several awards, Cook has completed two of her own books, *Exploring Mountain Highways* and *The Million Dollar Highway,* and has contributed to *Mother Earth: Through the Eyes of Women Photographers and Writers.* Kathleen Norris Cook makes her home in Colorado.

PAGE ii-iii—County road. San Juan Mts.

PAGE iv—Red leaves and birches. Split Rock S.P.

PAGE viii—Swift River fall colors.

PAGE 4—Autumn foliage.

PAGE 5—Redwoods. Jedediah Smith S.P.

PAGE 6-7—Winter tree study. Grand Mesa.

PAGE 13—Thunder Hole Area. Acadia N.P.

PAGE 17—Central California coast crashers.

PAGE 26-27—Autumn tree. Connecticut countryside.

PAGE 36—Gooseberry S.P., Lake Superior.

PAGE 40—Jackson Lake. Grand Tetons N.P.

PAGE 48—Owl Creek Pattern. San Juan Mts.

PAGE 49—Aspens. San Juan Mts.

PAGE 50-51—Sunset. Matzatzal Mts.

PAGE 52—Oak Creek ice study. Sedona area.

PAGE 60-61—Winter aspens and sunburst.

PAGE 96—Elves Chasm. Grand Canyon N.P.

PAGE 98-99—Snow showers at Hopi Point. Grand Canyon N.P.

PAGE 97—Colorado River at Saddle Mountain Area. Grand Canyon N.P.

PAT LEESON has been photographing wild places and wildlife for twenty years. From her home base in Vancouver, Washington, Leeson has traveled on assignment for the National Geographic Society and the National Wildlife Federation and has supplied images to America's leading corporations. Besides photographing two award-winning books on the American bald eagle with her photographer husband, Tom Leeson, her images have appeared in *On the Trail of the Desert Wildflower, Canyons of Color: Utah's Slickrock Wildlands* and *Yellowstone: Land of Fire and Ice.*

PAGE 8—Young hemlock among mature Douglas fir old growth.

PAGE 14—Vine maple leaves in fall grass. Western Washington.

PAGE 18—Western skunk cabbage after snowstorm.

PAGE 23—Wildflower display. W. Cascade Mts.

PAGE 70—Common woodfern and wood sorrel.

PAGE 82—Bald eagle feather.

PAGE 86—Sun shafts in forest.

PAGE 87—Sunset over fog.

PAGE 88—Small unnamed waterfall. Olympic N.P.

PAGE 89—Vine maple leaves on fallen log. Olympic N.P.

PAGE 90—Old-growth Douglas fir forest with young hemlock trees.

PAGE 91—Grass widows.

LONDIE PADELSKY is a professional photographer living in the mountains of the eastern Sierra near the town of Mammoth Lakes, California. Her work includes scenic landscapes from much of the western United States, including extensive work from the John Muir Wilderness. Londie Padelsky's images have appeared in many of America's leading travel and nature magazines and as fine art prints.

PAGE 44—Last light on sagebrush and Sierra Mts.

PAGE 45—Green rolling hills. Bridger-Teton N.F.

PAGE 77—Starfish on sand.

PAGE 78—Sand pattern.

PAGE 80-81—Atlantic Ocean from Cape May.

NANCY SIMMERMAN, a resident of Lummi Island, Washington, spends her life in the wilderness setting. A naturalist and photographer, Simmerman's travels take her throughout the Pacific Northwest. Her images have appeared in numerous magazines and books, including *Shadow of the Salmon.*

COVER—Mossy conifer rainforest, Glacier Bay N.P.

PAGE 12—Beach, Kukak Bay. Katmai N.M.

PAGE 15—Wind circles on beach. Lake Clark N.P.

PAGE 16—Sea, sand, sun, rock. Turnagain Arm.

PAGE 22—Mt. Sanford. Wrangell-St. Elias N.P.

PAGE 24—Salmonberry.

PAGE 25—Autumn colors: cottonwood, high-bush cranberry, alder.

PAGE 57—Snowden Mt. by midnight sun. Brooks Range.

PAGE 58—Wind-blown snow in March. White Pass.

PAGE 59—Snow, fog, trees. Muskeg Spaulding Meadows.

PAGE 68—Mt. Roberts Trail.

CONNIE TOOPS is a naturalist and freelance photojournalist whose images have appeared in the Audubon Society and Sierra Club calendars, in leading naturalist magazines, and in books published by the National Geographic Society, the National Wildlife Federation, Sierra Club, and others. Her own books include *National Seashores, Everglades,* and *Great Smoky Mountains.* Connie Toops makes her home in the Smoky Mountains of West Virginia.

PAGE 76—Ghost crab. Gulf Islands N.S.

PAGE 79—Saltmarsh. Assateague Is.